SAN JACINTO

WITHDRAWN

Library of Congress Cataloging-in-Publication Data

Pohl, James W., 1931–
  The Battle of San Jacinto.

  (Popular history series ; no. 3)
  1. San Jacinto, Battle of, 1836. I. Title. II. Series.
F390.P8 1989   976.4'03   89-4592
ISBN 0-87611-084-7

Cover: *Battle of San Jacinto, Texas* (detail) by L. M. D. Guillaume, ca. 1892.
Oil on canvas, 24 1/4 x 48 inches. *Courtesy of the R. W. Norton Art Gallery, Shreveport, La.*

THE BATTLE OF
SAN JACINTO

JAMES W. POHL

TEXAS STATE
HISTORICAL ASSOCIATION

THE BATTLE OF
SAN JACINTO

IN THE 1820S MANY PEOPLE CAME TO TEXAS, which was then part of Mexico. Many of these immigrants were from the United States. The lure of Texas was found in its vast quantity of good land amply watered by fourteen flowing rivers that nourished the soil as they rolled from the interior to the Gulf of Mexico. It was an agricultural age, and farmers knew that the key to personal and family prosperity lay in fertile soil.

Although President Thomas Jefferson consistently had held to the belief that Texas belonged to the United States through the provisions of the Louisiana Purchase (1803), the question of ownership shifted significantly in his lifetime. In 1819, for example, it appeared that the Adams–Onis Treaty ceded much of the land to Spain; however, the specific boundary line was never drawn, so the extent of sovereignty remained open to question. When Mexico gained its independence from Spain in 1821, the boundary matter remained unresolved, and no substantive agreement existed between the new country and the United States even into the 1830s. Nevertheless, it was generally accepted that some of the land known as Texas did, indeed, belong to Mexico.

These diplomatic matters meant very little, however, to the many colonists who were eager to begin their lives anew in what they regarded as a land of enormous promise. In an optimistic mood, they flocked to the land grant that had been given to the man who is called the Father of Texas, Stephen F. Austin. Pragmatic yet idealistic, Austin's own view of the diplomatic tangle was relatively simple. He accepted the fact that he and the rest of the newly arrived settlers, whether they had been American, English, German, or something else, were now loyal citizens of Mexico. His attitude in this matter was accepted by most of the people who joined him in Texas, and by the time of the Revolution, these new citizens exceeded the native Mexican population by a ratio of six to one.

Perhaps the most important reason for acceptance of new citizenship was the Constitution of Mexico, which dated from 1824; its provisions included a considerable measure of individual freedom by means of a liberal federal system of government. This happy situation changed dramatically, however, between the years 1833 and 1835. On a peaceful mission to Mexico City, Austin was seized and imprisoned under horrid conditions, on the baseless grounds that he was promoting insurrection and disobedience to the laws. When finally released after almost two years in prison, Austin returned to Texas a changed man. He concluded that Mexican authorities could never comprehend the basic tenets of constitutionalism together with its corollary, due process of law. In the wake of these events, he embraced the doctrines of revolution and independence. Again, his impressive influence swayed the minds of many Texans, who looked to him for leadership and admired him personally.

Austin's change was prompted in no small part by the seizure of power by the new Mexican president, Antonio López de Santa Anna Pérez de Lebrón, a thirty-nine-year-old opportunist with tyrannical tendencies. Santa Anna had begun his political and military career as a Spanish Royalist. But by the time of the Mexican Revolution, most people, including Texans, believed him when he said he was a convert to federalism. Upon his seizure of power, however, he became an unabashed Centralist, abrogated the excellent Constitution of 1824, supplanted it with a reactionary instrument, and assumed the role of dictator. He also had a cruel streak, evidenced by the savagery with which he suppressed a Federalist uprising in Zacatecas. It was in the wake

2

This image of Santa Anna appears in Don Lucas Alaman's *Historia de Mejico* (1852). Lithograph, 4 ³/₄ x 3 ¹/₂ inches (image). *Courtesy Benson Latin American Collection, The University of Texas at Austin.*

of these events that rebellion and the spirit of independence came alive in Texas.

The beautiful little city of Gonzales may claim to be the site of the first battle of the Texas Revolution, for near there on October 2, 1835, an engagement occurred between 160 determined Texan settlers and roughly 100 Mexican dragoons. This was ironic, because back in 1831 Mexico had given a small cannon to these same Texans for protection against Indians; but when relations between the settlers and the authorities steadily worsened, the cannon was reclaimed. There was no guarantee, after all, that it would not be used against Mexicans. That fear became reality when the defiant Gonzales Texans stood with their diminutive gun in the shadow of a two-staffed banner that held a representation of the cannon with the daring legend "Come and Take It." The Texans then fired a blast that drove off the troops. From that moment at Gonzales to the final day at San Jacinto, only six and a half months passed.

Because of Gonzales and another disturbance, this time at Anahuac, General Martín Perfecto de Cós landed at Copano Bay near Corpus Christi with a force of about 500 men and marched them from Copano Bay to San Antonio de Bexar, entering that city on October 9, 1835. Cós was a man of some importance—brother-in-law of Santa Anna—although he was an officer of limited abilities. There could be little doubt that the Texans were restless, for on the very next day the settlers seized the Presidio La Bahia at Goliad, where a Mexican constabulary was posted. In addition, Texan forces became involved in two other engagements and won both. One of these was the Grass Fight on October 28 just

The "Come and Take It" cannon. *Courtesy Texas Highways.*

Martin Perfecto de Cós. In *Pictorial History of Mexico and the Mexican War* (1869) by John Frost. Woodcut, 2 $^1/_4$ x 2 inches. *Courtesy Benson Latin American Collection, The University of Texas at Austin.*

outside San Antonio; the other was at the Mission Nuestra Senora de la Purisima Concepcion on November 26, also just outside the city.

While these events were taking place, a formal meeting of delegates from various Texas constituencies met at San Felipe de Austin in November, 1835. This Consultation, as it was called, issued a demand as well as a threat to the government of Mexico. First, it demanded the restoration of the decentralized Constitution of 1824 that Santa Anna had arbitrarily torn up; next, it declared that Texans would fight, if necessary, for their rights. It was at this emotional moment that a legendary figure appeared, a soldier with a magnetic personality who raised the cry, "Who will go with old Ben Milam to San Antonio?" At that defiant shout, 300 Texans rose up and marched on Bexar which had been besieged since October. After a stiff fight in which their leader lost

Sam Houston by Jesse H. Whitehurst, ca. 1845. Daguerrotype, half plate. *Courtesy Chicago Historical Society.*

his life, they seized the city on December 10, 1835. As a result of this humiliating defeat, General Cós was forced to take his troops out of Texas. It was a heady time, and the jubilant Texans exulted in their successes.

Their joy was short-lived, however, for by February of 1836, an angry and vindictive Santa Anna at the head of an army of about 5,000 men (it would eventually number nearly 8,000) crossed the Rio Grande near Laredo. He was not only Mexico's president but also its conquering general—used to crushing rebellions and determined to suppress this one. He vowed, if necessary, that he would employ even savage means to deal with the insurrection. With that grim warning, he declared all Texans under arms to be no more than pirates and swore that he would claim their lives if any were captured or caught in any act of rebellion.

As Santa Anna marched unimpeded toward San Antonio, farther to the east another Mexican military force, under the competent Mexican general José de Urrea, swept over small Texan forces at Agua Dulce, San Patricio, and Refugio. It was clear that Urrea was headed toward Goliad, which held about 500 Texans under the command of Colonel James Fannin, a soldier who had spent a few years at the United States Military Academy at West Point. It would have been a considerable benefit to the Texan cause had Sam Houston, named by the Consultation to the overall command of the Texas forces, assumed his authority at an early date. As Santa Anna's and Urrea's troops poured into Texas, however, Houston, known as Co-lo-neh, which in the Cherokee tongue means "the Raven," was in East Texas attempting to pacify the Indians. Texas, after all, could hardly fight a two-front war, one against the Mexicans and another against the Indians.

Despite a multitude of problems, Houston saw very early that the main fighting should take place in the eastern wooded area. Consequently, he ordered the remarkable Colonel James Bowie of the Texas militia to take command of the military forces at the Alamo near San Antonio de Bexar. The previous post commander, Lieutenant Colonel James Clinton Neill, would have left his position if he could have done so, but he realized that, if he did, the many artillery pieces that were located there would have to be abandoned. Neill simply did not have the horses or other draft animals necessary to remove the cannon. So there he sat—and so did the artillery. Bowie was ordered as early as December 15 and again on January 17 to destroy the Alamo; however, the famous knife fighter decided to ignore these directions and remain in San Antonio. For one thing, he was enamored of the thick walls, and he was loath to abandon the artillery. Earlier, at Concepción, Bowie had beaten a numerically superior force under the command of Cós without the advantages afforded by either walls or artillery, and he was eager to see how he might acquit himself now that he had both. If it occurred to him that he was disobeying orders, he did not seem to be troubled.

Meanwhile, Henry Smith, an early advocate of independence and acting governor of Texas, sent William Barret Travis, a young officer with leadership ability, to assume Neill's command at the Alamo. Travis also felt that the Alamo should be abandoned, for he shared Houston's assessment that San Antonio and its defenses were simply too far west to be an effective barrier against a huge invading army. In fact, at one point Travis even declared that San Antonio was "the enemy's country." Once on the scene, however, he also was impressed by the thick walls and the abundant cannon, and reversed his position. The Alamo, he declared, was "the key to Texas." Bowie and Travis, now in joint command, disagreed on many issues, but they were of like mind on the value of their fortified position. They would stand at the Alamo with about 150 men. In time, they were joined by more than 30 others from Gonzales, and, Travis assumed, hundreds of additional Texans would reinforce him.

When Santa Anna arrived with his large body of men in San Antonio on February 23, 1836, he quickly decided that the Alamo should be assaulted. For thirteen days he set about positioning his troops, moving a number forward by trenches, placing artillery at critical points, and considering the use of scaling ladders. Finally, just before dawn on March 6, Santa Anna struck the Texan defenses. After a bloody two-hour ordeal, which included much hand-to-hand combat, the massive Mexican weight overcame stubborn Texan resistance. In the end, all the defenders were killed and their bodies callously burned. Only women, children, and black slaves were spared. Among the few survivors was Susannah Dickinson, wife of Alamo defender Alamaron Dickinson. It was she, with an infant daughter in her arms, who carried the news of the ghastly slaughter to Sam Houston at Gonzales.

Houston took command of his troops on March 11. Up to this time he had been a general only on paper. His imposing title was commander-in-chief of the army, which summed up his duties fairly well; he was in charge of all regulars, volunteers, and militia. But his position in the field fell far short of the description.

On occasion he simply was not obeyed, for he was in command of rough and independent-minded men who did not follow orders easily. The stubborn Jim Bowie was a case in point; James Fannin would provide another example. Houston ordered Fannin to join him in all haste. After all, Houston had only about 370 men at Gonzales, and he could hardly turn back the Mexican army with such a small band of volunteers.

When Susannah Dickinson arrived in Gonzales and told of the horror at the Alamo, the townspeople were stunned. Their fathers, sons, and brothers would not return; they had died within the mission walls. Shock gave way to grief. Houston, on whose broad shoulders lay the responsibility for the defense of Texas, was also stunned, but neither he nor the citizens of Gonzales could lament for long because Mrs. Dickinson brought other news as well. Generalissimo Santa Anna himself, at the head of thousands, was heading in their direction and soon would fall on Gonzales and East Texas.

Quickly recovering, Houston sent word to the Texas government at Washington-on-the-Brazos. He would have to withdraw until he could meet the numerically superior Mexicans at a more advantageous position. Houston's movements were logical; there simply was no way that he could match his Mexican opponent. His few hundred half-trained men with poor arms were insufficient for such a task. The disparity in the sizes of the opposing forces called for a particular stratagem, and Houston had one.

He would withdraw as far as necessary—but, he hoped, not too far. He assumed, of course, that he soon would be reinforced by the garrison from Goliad somewhere in the vicinity of Cibolo Creek. Then he would begin hitting the Mexican forces. These considerations, generally understood by all, were swept away, and Houston's hopes were dashed when it was learned that Fannin, while executing a poor maneuver, had quit Goliad and allowed his command to be caught in the open near Coleto Creek. Out of food and water and heavily outnumbered by Mexican troops under the command of the able Urrea, Fannin had surrendered under what he considered honorable terms. When the Texans were marched back to Goliad, however, Urrea's humane terms were countermanded.The captured troops, crammed into a stifling chapel, had been told to expect repatriation. Instead, Santa Anna ordered the entire Texan command killed in cold blood. A few physicians were spared, and a few other soldiers escaped to tell the dreadful tale.

Thus, the tragedy of the Alamo was compounded by the tragedy of Goliad. Houston now faced insuperable odds. He could no longer merely withdraw and wait for reinforcements— only escape could save the tiny Texas army from extermination. It was no longer withdrawal; it was retreat, a full-scale dash for safety.

Even before the news of the Goliad disaster arrived, Houston had turned over to the desperate residents of Gonzales three of his four supply wagons to help them as they began their flight toward the Sabine. It was all he could spare, and he could ill afford the loss of those. This left him with no means of transporting his cannon, which, with immense regret, he sank to the bottom of the rain-swollen Guadalupe River. The weather had been unusually se-vere that spring, and the rain poured incessantly even as the foaming stream swallowed the pieces.

The flight of the people of Gonzales marked the beginning of the Runaway Scrape—hundreds of civilians, eager to escape the wrath of Santa Anna, fleeing pell-mell northward and eastward. In time the hundreds became thousands. Gonzales was burned to the ground. No one knows who gave the order. Houston was accused of it, but he denied having issued the command. In any event, the flames did their work, ensuring that the site was rendered useless to Santa Anna. Only cold ashes remained—and the cold hatred of the Texans, who longed to avenge Santa Anna's atrocities, was born. In the midst of this chaos, a somewhat des-perate Houston lunged toward the Colorado River.

There are those who maintain that Houston hoped the pursu-ing Mexicans would outrun their supplies. But it must also be noted that he was simply running—for the life of his army, and the Revolution, and Texas. One more incident like the Alamo or Goliad, and the struggle would be over. Furthermore, he knew that the population center of the Anglo-American settlement lay in East Texas. There, amid the deep forests and in friendly recruiting territory, he would meet the Mexicans on what he only could hope would be more nearly equal terms.

The very day after Houston quit Gonzales, Santa Anna learned of it, delighted that his quarry was flushed. Accordingly, he planned to attack the very heart of the Texan settlement. His scheme called for three separate columns, one under General Antonio Gaona striking to the northeast; General Joaquín Ramírez y Sesma, trailing Houston in a central thrust; and General José de Urrea, moving up from the south. Santa Anna stayed near Gonzales with troops held by his second-in-command, General Vicente Filisola.

Santa Anna adopted a curious and rather casual attitude toward the pursuit. It seems he believed the war was over. His subordinates became disturbed by his demeanor, which could only be described as a mixture of arrogance and disdain. Nevertheless, it must be noted that this movement was competently executed, and it may well have been Santa Anna's best action in the war. In essence, he planned to trap Houston, to squeeze him like a nut in a nutcracker. Santa Anna pompously viewed himself as the "Napoleon of the West." In retrospect, the comparison is absurd, but this particular thrust did have some Napoleonic qualities—especially the flanking aspect, which compares favorably with Bonaparte's efforts at Marengo and Jena.

Houston, who had no formal military education, was nevertheless a reasonably good strategist and immediately perceived his own dilemma. No matter which way he turned, he could be brought to battle by one of Santa Anna's columns, any of which was larger than his own. If one of them caught him, the other two would move in like wolves circling a cornered stag. That is why Houston headed north. By March 17 the little band reached the Colorado and set up bivouac at Burnham's Crossing. By March 19 Houston prodded it across the still swollen waters and set up camp at Beason's Ford near the present-day site of Columbus. By that time the depredations of Santa Anna had become more generally known, and the Runaway Scrape had become a steady stream of fugitives, some old and sick, some mere children.

Henry Smith was no longer the governor. The president of the newly proclaimed Republic of Texas was David G. Burnet; together with Secretary of War Thomas J. Rusk, he called for the people to stand and fight. Some were afraid, but a thirst for vengeance struck others, and Houston's army began to swell. By the time Houston reached the Colorado he had 600 men, and by the time he reached Burnham's Crossing he probably had a few more. On March 20 Ramírez y Sesma and his 800 men touched the west bank of the Colorado. Over the next few days the Mexican commander looked for a ford without success. All the while Houston's band grew to well over 1,000 strong. But even then Houston did not attack, though it is generally believed that his force eventually numbered 1,400 men, the largest number he commanded in the entire war. Instead, he withdrew all the way to San Felipe de Austin on the Brazos River.

During this retreat, elements in his command became increasingly unruly. On learning that their number actually exceeded that of Ramírez y Sesma and that Houston still showed no inclination toward meeting his adversary, the Texans began to grumble—and shortly thereafter about 200 men deserted the ranks. Some left in anger, others because they were determined to fight even if their commander chose to wait.

Two of those who left in order to fight the Mexicans independently were captains Wylie Martin and Moseley Baker. Both men utterly refused to take part in the further retrograde movement that Houston had planned. At this point Houston decided to move from San Felipe to Groce's Plantation, again out of the direct path of his pursuers. Rather than acknowledge what now amounted to open insubordination, and thus a practical disavowal of his very command, Houston gave these malcontents vague orders that corresponded with their wishes. In essence, he told them to act as the security for his rear and to guard against advancing Mexicans.

Why did Houston continue his retreat even though his forces outnumbered those of Ramírez y Sesma? Because Santa Anna was moving by divisions, which could provide fast reinforcement. Of course, there was a risk for the Mexicans as well. The terrible weather might well delay a timely linking. There was still another reason for Houston's reluctance to attack. As far as could be determined, Santa Anna was in command of a reasonably disciplined force, whose columns possessed both cavalry and artillery. Even if Houston's undisciplined volunteers somehow managed to face the foe, they would have to do so as light infantrymen. Houston simply did not have additional weapons or units. In short, he felt that his force did not have either the strength or the discipline to take the offensive. Under these conditions, the defeat of his enemy either in mass or in detail was just not a reasonable expectation.

Houston would have to wait even longer before he could hope for success. In fact, he was still without ordnance. It is not that he failed to recognize the value of artillery—he simply did not have it, and even if he had, he did not have the means to haul it overland. He would accept artillery if he could get it, and he would even try to drag it with him. He made arrangements with William T. Austin for the procurement of two pieces, but the miserable weather again made the acquisition difficult.

Nevertheless, for failing to attack Ramírez y Sesma, he was severely criticized not only by many within his army but also without. President Burnet castigated him and stopped just short of calling him a coward. "The enemy are laughing you to scorn," he angrily wrote to Houston, "you must fight them." By this time the government of Texas had fled from the capital at Washington-on-the-Brazos toward the Gulf coast at Harrisburg (today near the site of Houston). Never an admirer of his general, even after the war, Burnet wrote scathingly, "Sam Houston has been generally acclaimed the hero of San Jacinto. No fiction of the novelist is farther from the truth. Houston was the only man on the battlefield who deserved censure. The army regarded him as a military fop, and the citizens were disgusted at his miserable imbecility." Throughout this ordeal Houston, though frayed at times, kept a reasonable humor, sardonically describing the government's scramble to Harrisburg as "the flight of the wise men." In a mood of some annoyance, however, he wrote to his friend Thomas Rusk, "The retreat of the government will have a bad effect on the troops." Later, in a worse temper, he wrote, "Oh, why did the cabinet leave Washington?"

By this time Houston, fearing the worst—that his army might fall victim to even greater desertion—resorted to a ruse. After dispatching a courier to carry his letters to the secretary of war, he suddenly called him back. Taking a pencil from his worn coat, he indicated that he needed to add one more note. He scrawled a message on the folder to the effect that reinforcements would soon bring his strength to 1,500 men. To be sure, that note was pure nonsense, but Houston knew that the courier would pass on the misinformation and that a rumor would run through the camp like wildfire. This bit of psychology did help to lessen the desertion rate. But there was even more ominous news. Santa Anna's army had grown to about 8,000 men.

Even if the president and some of the soldiers lacked confidence in his abilities, Houston doggedly held to his overall plan. He was no longer retreating just for the sake of retreating—he was past that stage. He knew that he commanded, if that was even the proper word, a motley band; the men were unskilled and untutored in the rudiments of nineteenth-century warfare. That meant that they had to be trained. No soldier truly enjoys drill, and cantankerous volunteers hate it more than others. Nevertheless, at Groce's Plantation, Houston drilled them. To the disenchanted soldiers, it seemed as if the drill would never end, but Houston was adamant. They would at least learn the basics: to form a line, to fire by volley, to advance by quickstep. Although in some volunteers' minds, Houston the unready now also became Houston the martinet. But he did make soldiers of them, and they did learn the most fundamental aspects of contemporary battle formation.

The views of his detractors notwithstanding, Houston had not lost his nerve. Rather, he was simply unwilling to risk both his army and his country on a roll of the dice. Also, from that time forward, Houston increasingly kept his own counsel, confiding in no one his intentions toward his adversary. He felt that he could cope with the rebellious attitude of his troops better than he could with their disappointment. So, despite growing resentment in the ranks, Houston held firm, his will as resolute as a compass needle.

One historian wrote of this episode that "it is one of the finest examples in history where one man pitted his will against that of the mob, and, although the loser on several occasions, finally won out."

The reference to the "mob" may not be too wide of the mark. Travis, the defender of the Alamo, also referred to the Texan soldiers of the Revolution with that same term. In fairness, the soldiers' attitudes were molded by the conditions in which they found themselves. It was, after all, an extremely wet spring, and the normally balmy days were punctuated by repeated northers. Hardly a day passed without a cold rain that pelted the men mercilessly. Their commander could be seen, his hat pulled nearly to his ears, sitting with no protection other than a drenched blanket. It could not have been an inspiring sight. Before long the pestilence of dysentery crept into this dank, unhealthy climate and stalked the men. So there Houston sat at Groce's Plantation, ceaselessly drilling an angry, wet, sick little army, defying its demands, distrusted by his own president, and utterly alone in the spreading gloom. It is a cliché that command is a lonely business, but nowhere is that more evident than in Houston's solitary setting.

By April 17 Santa Anna, at the head of 1,400 troops, reached the burnt-out remains of San Felipe. On the whole, he was pleased with his success up to that point, for he had marched halfway from San Antonio to the Gulf of Mexico and had encountered no serious opposition. Fortunately for Houston, the rear guard of Baker and Martin had met the Mexicans. These Texans picked their positions well, even to the point of constructing trenches, so it required some time for the Mexicans to uproot them and to resume the pursuit.

Santa Anna soon learned that Burnet and the Texas government had fled from Washington-on-the Brazos to Harrisburg. The generalissimo immediately determined that he should march on the town in order to capture the government and, simultaneously, to demonstrate his ease of movement over the enemy's countryside. It seemed reasonable, but it was, perhaps, the fundamental error of his campaign. He already had divided his forces, a proper move in view of the fact that he hoped by combined maneuver to track down Houston. His strike toward Harrisburg, however, involved two miscalculations. First, he lost sight of his original objective, which was to capture or to destroy Houston; second, he divided his forces even further so that he no longer moved in strength at critical points. If these misjudgments were not enough, he compounded them by deciding to ride at the head of his small detached force. Should he be captured or otherwise incapacitated, what would happen to his Texas campaign? Apparently, this possibility never entered Santa Anna's head.

Earlier Santa Anna had no intention of leading the Harrisburg expedition. He changed his mind in part because of news from Mexico City. Vice-president Miguel Barragán, a loyal supporter and acting president of Mexico in Santa Anna's absence, had died. Although still president, Santa Anna was by no means certain that his political strength remained as secure at home as it had been before the start of the Texas campaign. He thought of quickly returning; but in order to do that, he would have to go by sea— and the Texas navy, in command of the coast, had managed to take his vessel out of commission. Under the circumstances, Santa Anna decided to see the war to its conclusion, whereupon he would return via an overland route, his success in battle a prop both to his title of president and to his future ambitions.

This political development may have left the president a bit nervous. After all, previous Mexican governments—and he had lived through several of them—were not known for their stability. It may have been that Barragan's death was the catalyst for Santa Anna's increasingly erratic attitude toward the conduct of the Texas campaign, which he now seemed suddenly anxious to end.

Of course, at this same time, Sam Houston could not begin to know what enormous services had been rendered him both by Barragan's death and by the Texas navy. He was still involved in a struggle to retain his authority. The distrust from both his men and his superiors had caused him, only days before, to write to his friend the secretary of war, Thomas Rusk, "On my arrival at the Brazos, had I consulted the wishes of all, I should have been like an ass between two stacks of hay. Many wished me to go below, others above. I consulted none—I held no councils of war. If I err, the blame is mine."

Despite these brave words, Houston did have to accommodate his command on one point. He had to assure them that his ultimate intention was to meet and to destroy the enemy even, in the general's phrase, if the odds were "ten to one" in Santa Anna's favor. All the while at Groce's Plantation the black skies grew blacker, the rain fell in sheets, and new sicknesses came calling. To the already debilitating dysentery were added measles and whooping cough. By now the disgruntled Burnet considered replacing his reluctant commander with Secretary Rusk and even sent the secretary to Houston's camp with orders to exercise his discretion in the matter. Fortunately for Houston, Rusk was a confident and loyal friend, but despite Rusk's sympathies, the situation was clear: Houston simply had to meet the enemy soon or face disgrace.

One of those who shared Burnet's doubts was a newly arrived young soldier from Georgia, Mirabeau Bonaparte Lamar, a man of intense ambition. Immediately upon his arrival, Lamar exerted his influence over others. This in itself might have been admirable, except that his own considerable leadership qualities all seemed to be aimed at the denigration of Houston. Had it been possible to wrest Houston's command from him, he might well have tried. At one point, for example, when Houston's army had risen to about 800 men, Lamar wanted to take nearly half of them, as well as the steamer *Yellowstone* (the army's principal logistical support line) for the purpose of conducting guerrilla raids. Lamar wanted this despite the fact that he was enlisted as a private soldier. Houston soon came to view Lamar as a parvenu and a climber. The younger man had come to Texas only after a series of disappointments that included two congressional defeats. Despite his low rank in the Texan army, Lamar's star would rise dramatically at San Jacinto.

Another who doubted Houston's leadership was the fiery Kentuckian Sidney Sherman, who even entertained dark thoughts that his general was motivated by cowardice. He came from his

Mirabeau B. Lamar, ca. 1845. Daguerrotype, half plate.
Courtesy San Jacinto Museum of History.

home state at the head of a company. At Gonzales he had been raised to the command of a regiment. On the Colorado, Colonel Sherman had demanded the right to attack Ramírez y Sesma. When permission was denied, he questioned Houston's fitness for the job—like Lamar, he would not have shrunk from taking over the entire army. For his part, Houston appreciated Sherman's ardor, but also regarded him with suspicion and came to look on the Kentuckians as rowdies. It was these men who carried the Kentucky-made flag that the Texans flew at San Jacinto.

In time the discontented raised such a cry that Houston feared for the very existence of his small army. If those demanding separate and independent expeditions had been given their way, the force would have utterly disintegrated. To forestall such a possibility, Houston posted notices in and about the campsite to the effect that the first man to raise volunteers for any such purpose would be subject to court-martial and subsequent death by firing squad. It was a leaf taken from the book of his old commander, Andrew Jackson. This public firmness had the desired effect, and the cry for separate military adventures soon died out.

Helping to drown the cacophony of disruption was Tom Rusk, who had recently traded his cabinet post for a colonel's command. The importance of his timely arrival in Houston's camp in early April and his solid and obvious support cannot be overes-

Sidney Sherman by unknown artist, 1835. Oil on canvas, 33 × 38 inches. *Courtesy San Jacinto Museum of History.*

The San Jacinto Battle Flag carried by the Texans. 46 x 50 inches. Decorated with the image of Liberty, this flag was made by the women of Newport, Kentucky, who presented it to Sidney Sherman's volunteer company of soldiers raised in that town. Today it is displayed in the Capitol in Austin. *Courtesy Archives Division, Texas State Library.*

timated. Even John Wharton, an adjutant general and an early supporter of Houston, had begun to wonder if his commander were up to the task. Still, Wharton could be relied upon, for the time being at least, to be a steadying influence. One more remained unshaken in his loyalty to Houston, Colonel Edward Burleson, commander of the First Regiment. Through the efforts of Burleson and Rusk, and to some extent Wharton, Houston was able to maintain a reasonably effective command.

At this point , Houston finally received some good news. Santa Anna had held a council of war at Elizabeth Powell's inn on the San Bernard River. Mrs. Powell's son understood Spanish and learned that Santa Anna would lead a column to the Harrisburg area. This information was immediately relayed to Houston. It was the best of news, for Houston now determined to cross the Brazos with the help of the *Yellowstone*. He remained secretive, as usual, and his soldiers were still unsure if he meant to attack Santa Anna. Nevertheless, they were moving, albeit slowly, for it took two days to cross the turbulent river.

After crossing the Brazos, the army received another boon. The citizens of Cincinnati, Ohio, stung by news of the Alamo and Goliad and in deepest sympathy with the ideals of the Revolution, demonstrated their support by sending a matched pair of six-pounders. The cannon came by way of the Ohio and Mississippi rivers, thence from New Orleans and up from Harrisburg. Fortunately, Houston had two officers who knew how to use them. James Neill, the man who had cared for the ordnance at the Alamo before Travis's arrival, was with Houston, along with a thirty-four-year-old Philadelphian, George Washington Hockley, who also served as Houston's chief of staff. Each piece required a crew of nine, but more than twice that many volunteered to be artillerymen.

The question must arise as to why Houston, who had previously abandoned artillery, would be so pleased to received these pieces. After all, the weather still was miserable, the roads still were knee-deep in mud, and the transport of the cannon still would be enormously difficult. The answer is, the nature of the war had now changed. For those who might wonder if Houston truly desired the offensive, it is necessary to consider his attitude toward these fieldpieces. Offensive warfare demanded these weapons, and this time—in spite of rain, mud, or whatever—Houston would haul the cannon, if necessary, on the backs of his men. That fact was dramatized by the widely published story of the encounter between Houston and Mrs. Pamela Mann. Mrs. Mann had allowed her yoke of oxen to pull the artillery only as far as suited her convenience. When Houston indicated that the oxen would be commandeered for the remainder of the trip eastward, the feisty woman uttered an oath, branded the general a liar, and, brandishing a large blade, cut her animals free from their tethers and led them off. When the lead teamster complained to Houston that "we can't get along without them oxen; the cannon is done bogged down," Houston's only reply was a blunt, "Well, we have to get along as best we can." This time the "Twin Sisters," as the army called the cannon, would not be left behind.

The army's displacement across the Brazos and the subsequent march to the east did not convince everyone in Houston's army that the general actually was moving against the Mexicans. The lingering suspicions may be seen in Moseley Baker's newest defiant refusal to serve directly under Houston. If Houston had acted unwisely in the face of this threat, a bad situation could have become worse. Rather than punish the recalcitrant soldier, an act he knew would damage morale, Houston shrewdly ordered Baker and his men to the Trinity River, ostensibly to aid civilians still caught in the Runaway Scrape. In reality, he was just getting rid of one more troublemaker. Houston could have used Baker and his band, but he did not need their endless bickering and insubordination. As it turned out, Baker returned in time to participate in the battle of San Jacinto.

Even with Baker's removal, doubts remained. Would Houston really move toward Harrisburg and against the Mexicans? Although the little army was on the road that might eventually lead to Harrisburg, that road led other places as well. The left fork that the men would reach after only a few days' march went north to Nacogdoches; the right fork went east to Harrisburg. Characteristically, Houston gave not the slightest hint of his intentions, even though he knew of an impending mutiny if the army veered left.

As the men reached the fork, some of them milled about a bit, but the more determined swung to the right; and in the end, the main body followed. The debate remains: did the army decide for Houston or did it simply do what Houston had already decided? Did Houston, by seeming to let the army choose its own fate, also allow the psychology of the situation to work in his favor? That is, by allowing free choice of the right, did he produce a grim determination in the force's collective mind—that the future held nothing less than victory or death—a point that he himself would

Erastus "Deaf" Smith by T. Jefferson Wright, 1936. Oil on canvas, 33 × 38 inches. *Courtesy San Jacinto Museum of History.*

later make before the battle? These questions can never be answered with certainty. Even after the battle, various interpretations were given, many, of course, dependent upon the opinion of the speculator. Houston, in perfect keeping with his stoic demeanor on the march, made no specific reference to them.

The army no longer doubted where it was going; it was to meet the Mexicans somewhere around Harrisburg. With the march to the right, the entire character of the army seemed to change. What had been a slow-paced, and even casual, campaign was now an obsessive and frenzied drive as Houston's speed began to approximate that of a forced march. They wanted to fight Mexicans? They wanted blood? Well, by thunder, Houston was determined that they would have what they desired, and he whipped them forward in the still foul weather.

Despite the constant rain, interminable muck, scant and soggy food, continually wet clothes and skin, the army pressed on. By April 18 it had reached Harrisburg, where it virtually collapsed for a brief rest. It had moved about sixty miles in just two days under daunting conditions. At the same time, however, it had a great stroke of luck. Houston had ordered out a reconnaissance party headed by Erastus "Deaf" Smith, a native New Yorker, who, along with Henry Karnes, was the best of his scouts. Smith and Karnes intercepted two Mexican messengers, one of whom carried the saddlebags of the martyred Travis, his name stamped on them for all the world to see. The situation played into Houston's hands—his troops, already spoiling for a fight, were roused to fury.

Of even greater importance were the contents of the bags, for the messages revealed that a Mexican force of only about 800 lay before them, commanded by the executioner of Travis—Santa Anna himself. The messages also revealed that reinforcements might soon arrive, but for Houston the news was almost too good to be true. He realized that for the first time in this struggle he could not only meet the enemy on approximately equal terms but also, if successful, could seize the president of Mexico, to whom he could dictate the terms of peace.

Thus it was that an emboldened and rejuvenated Houston appeared before an assembly of his troops in the early hours of April 19. Both he and Rusk addressed the men. Houston spoke first: "The army will cross and will meet the enemy. Some of us may be killed and must be killed; but, soldiers, remember the Alamo, the Alamo! the Alamo!" It was precisely the speech to inflame the spirits of already determined men. They set their jaws and vowed to destroy the enemy. One of those present said ominously that from that point on he knew "damned few will be taken prisoners." Sam Houston gave more than a speech that day—he gave the very battle cry of the Texas Revolution.

Santa Anna, meanwhile, exuded overconfidence. This day was no different than the rest. After the Alamo, he was sure that the

Juan N. Almonte, ca. 1860. Photograph on carte de visite, 2 ³/₄ x 1 ³/₄ inches (image). *Courtesy Benson Latin American Collection, The University of Texas at Austin.*

rebellion was all but crushed, and it took the best combined efforts of his officers to convince him to remain in Texas to see the effort through. It seems as though he had difficulty fixing on the objective of the campaign. It should have been clear that it was essential to overwhelm the opposition, and that mission could only be accomplished by crushing Houston's army, for as long as there was organized resistance in Texas, the war would not come to an end. Surely, someone coming from a revolutionary background and strife-torn country such as Santa Anna should have understood that fact.

As he moved eastward, however, Santa Anna hit upon another

scheme. Among the smoldering ashes of San Felipe, Santa Anna had discovered the whereabouts of Burnet and his cabinet. Inasmuch as his prey was a mere thirty miles beyond the Fort Bend Crossing on the Brazos, the Mexican general decided that he would track it down. Instead of simply defeating Houston, he would also capture the rebel government. This threat so disturbed President Burnet that he, vice-president Lorenzo de Zavala, and the rest of the government fled to Harrisburg. Almost immediately Santa Anna made another error. If he had moved at once and ridden through the darkness, there is every reason to believe that the capture would have been effected. Instead, he ordered Ramírez y Sesma forward after a linkup with the advancing Filisola. Only then did Santa Anna and about 900 men set out for Harrisburg.

Santa Anna soon discovered to his disgust that the delay had permitted Burnet and the others to flee again, this time toward New Washington. In his fury at failing to bag his bird, Santa Anna burned Harrisburg, destroyed the newspaper that had just printed the Texas Declaration of Independence, and sent his trusted and able subordinate Colonel Juan N. Almonte at the head of fifty dragoons speeding toward New Washington. It was a narrow escape for Burnet. The president, his wife, and the cabinet were barely able to leap into a rowboat and pull away from the pier as Almonte arrived. The Mexican soldiers immediately began a fusillade, but the gentlemanly Almonte realized that a woman was aboard the tiny craft and would not tolerate further fire. Thus, the government escaped by way of a woman's farthingale and eventually found safe haven on Galveston Island. It crossed Burnet's mind to proceed to New Orleans. He did not do so, but Almonte reported such a move to Santa Anna.

Apart from this quixotic and failed enterprise, there was still the main problem—Houston's army—to which Santa Anna almost casually turned his hand. Knowing Houston's general direction and his presumed route of march, Santa Anna decided to make for Lynch's Ferry on the banks of the San Jacinto River. The Ferry could be approached by two roads, one from New Washington and the other from Harrisburg, which merged close to the ferry.

On the opposite northeastern shore was the village of Lynchburg, and from there the road continued in a northeasterly direction before turning south toward Anahuac. Santa Anna proceeded through the general area of the west bank hoping to meet the Texans, probably beyond Lynchburg, and at the same time to cut off their line of retreat. Once again, he was entirely too optimistic.

It is curious that Houston, who was camped at White Oak Bayou across from the ruins of Harrisburg, looked upon the situation somewhat similarly. On the morning of April 20 Houston awakened his troops. It did not require much of an effort to rouse them. Few had slept the night before; it had been particularly cold, with another late norther blowing in. The men lifted themselves in their soggy clothes from the dew-dampened earth. Most of them had gone without supper the night before, but they knew that Mexican soldiers were in the area, so they sprang to their feet.

The army was not at full strength; roughly 250 of Houston's men were sick and had been left with the logistical stores near what remained of Harrisburg. As the chilling dawn reached out in streaks, the men were on the march. They rested long enough to start a coarse breakfast mainly of beef, the result of the sacrifice of three cows that belonged to a rancher in the area. These were not the kind of men to let a brand stand in the way of an empty belly.

Their meal was interrupted by excited scouts who rushed into camp with news that Mexicans were close at hand. Hearing the story, several hundred of the men discharged their weapons. Astounded that his men would so wantonly disclose their position to the enemy, Houston bawled for silence, even threatening on one occasion to run his sword through the next man who fired his piece. His raging anger and profane threats did no good at all, and the soldiers looked upon them as mere bluff and bluster. They wanted to clear their weapons by blowing away the wetness, and no mere commanding general could tell them no. Houston, exasperated, remembered the type of troops he commanded and just gave up the effort. Incredibly, the Mexicans did not hear the shooting.

On the march again, the disorderly troops saw a wisp of smoke in the distance. Houston wondered aloud if it was a prairie fire, but soon perceived it to be New Washington in flames. Santa Anna had burned the town before setting out for Lynch's Ferry. He had no idea, of course, that Houston and his men were already there.

The field on which the two armies would meet was, for all practical purposes, on a promontory facing north-northeast, which jutted out into a rather large body of water. On one side was Buffalo Bayou, which fell away to the southwest. Buffalo Bayou's confluence with the San Jacinto River was the distinguishing feature, and the river flowed to the southeast. Several other significant bodies of water were adjacent to these large streams, the most important being Peggy's Lake, which gave the appearance of a small bay located on the western bank of the river. Peggy's Lake helped the land take on its peninsular appearance. All around the head and edges of the promontory was marshland; but as one traveled a bit inland, only a score of yards, one found rather large groves of live oak, often intermingled with other timber. Similar land was found down Buffalo Bayou. In front of the grove of trees on the Buffalo Bayou side stretched the Harrisburg Road, which also led to Vince's Bridge. Going in the opposite direction, the road abruptly stopped at water's edge. That is where Lynch's Ferry, from which the point received its name, began. So marshland and timbered groves lined the promontory; but as soon as one emerged from the stand of trees, one came onto a large and magnificent plain of grass. This grass rolled on, about a mile, from north to south, perhaps several miles from east to west. It was no accident that the battle took place on the narrowest part of the field, because the country was made to order for it.

It was ten in the morning when Houston spread his ragged band amid the dense live oak grove that ran along Buffalo Bayou. Before him stretched the open field with grass rising taller than a man's boot. It was on that same plain that surprised Mexican scouts caught their first glimpse of the Texan pickets. They quickly spurred their animals to another grove farther to the south. The Texans remained concealed and did not expose themselves. Santa Anna knew by now, however, that he had stumbled upon the main body of the Texas army and that it was already at Lynch's Ferry.

By one o'clock in the afternoon Sidney Sherman, who had been on reconnaissance duty, returned with information that the enemy's horse soldiers were only about a mile away. No sooner had he uttered these words than dragoons drew up before the Texans. At this point Houston ordered his men to lie down; he was determined to conceal both the size of his small army and the weapons at his disposal. About sixty men huddled together in an attempt to mask the cannon. The dragoons approached, fearlessly it seemed to some of the Texans, accompanied by the shrill and penetrating blare of the bugles. The blast had its desired effect, for some of the Texans later reported that this particular episode was the most unnerving part of the entire campaign.

Houston, himself uneasy, turned to Isaac N. Moreland, who as a captain of the regular artillery inherited the role of chief of artillery from the ailing Neill. Moreland indicated that the sights were too high and the time was not yet right for firing. Nevertheless, eager to draw blood, Houston called out in a loud voice, "Clear the guns and fire!" The guns did not fire. But Houston's booming voice seemed to work—the dragoons stopped and then suddenly retired to the main body. A rumble of annoyance swept through the Texan ranks. What was wrong with the cannon? To add to the consternation, almost immediately the Mexicans rolled a fieldpiece forward. There is some debate as to its size, but Dr. Nicholas D. Labadie, a Canadian surgeon and enthusiastic supporter of the Revolution, claimed it was a twelve-pounder. It has otherwise been described as the Golden Standard.

No matter what its size or its name, it was fired; immediately, deadly grapeshot fell into the tree line. Fortunately for the Texans, the gun's elevation was too high. This time the Texan artillery responded. Some say both Twin Sisters answered, others say only one fired. In any event, the Mexicans withdrew, but not all the way to the main body. By then it was four o'clock, and the Mexican cannon still was not altogether secure, so Sherman urged Houston to let him try to seize it. He had some horses, and he argued persuasively that he could surely beat off a counterattack by Mexican cavalry and bring back the cannon all in one great swoop. Debate followed with Houston not altogether favoring this bravado, but in the end he granted permission. It would give the insistent Sherman something to do, and if he could pull it off, the cannon would be a prize. Just as Sherman and 70 volunteers were about to move out, the Mexicans suddenly recalled their cannon. Undeterred, Sherman, Lamar, and others charged the position anyway. It was a gallant but foolish gesture. The Texans were not really cavalry at all but merely mounted riflemen. After their initial assault, which netted nothing, they were forced to retire in order to reload. Reloading also meant dismounting, whereupon the Mexican cavalry, seizing the opportunity, launched its own counterassault. As the Mexican horsemen charged, several hundred foot soldiers followed, while the Mexican cannon rained shot on Sherman's men. All the while, the enemy bugle blasted a warning—"No quarter!" Instead of immediately withdrawing to safety, Sherman stubbornly retained his poor position; to compound his error, he ordered a reserve contingent forward from the tree line. Houston would not hear of it. By that time he had his belly full of Sherman. He had not cared for the idea of a helter-skelter attack in the first place, and certainly he did not approve of it after its cause, the artillery, had been removed. Houston was not about to be drawn into an extended engagement brought on by an overly enthusiastic commander and fought on Mexican terms.

What Houston's decision amounted to was clear: Sherman and his lads would have to find their way back the best way they could. They did fight through to the lines, but not before losing several horses and having three men wounded. Lamar's heroism was conspicuous. Not only did he drag back two wounded comrades, but he also killed one of the enemy at close range while doing so. For his day's performance, the Georgian was given the rank of colonel and command of the Texas cavalry. Still, Houston's cold-blooded detachment combined with his inaction rankled, and Sherman never forgave his commander. That ended the fighting for April 20. Each side pulled back to its original position and awaited developments. Even so, there were some Texans who still clamored for renewed action that very day.

It is not altogether clear why Houston did not immediately go over to the offensive, rather than waiting. One can only surmise his thoughts. Perhaps he felt because of the day's action that the element of surprise was gone and therefore preferred to reconsider his options. Maybe he was wondering how he might regain surprise or was weighing the merits of a defensive as opposed to an offensive battle. He may have been considering all these things as well as others.

It seems fairly clear, however, that he was mulling over the possibility of a defense. After all, he had a choice. He could move against the enemy or he could have the enemy move against him. It was a defensive position similar to this one that helped Jim Bowie defeat the Mexicans at Concepción, and it is axiomatic that in war defense is stronger than offense. That being the case, why not let Santa Anna attack in order to offset the imbalance of numbers? Houston was not a trained soldier, but he had experienced combat, distinguishing himself in the Creek War at the battle of Horseshoe Bend. In that particular engagement, Andrew Jackson's attack was slowed by an Indian defensive position based on a modified British fortification. So there seems to be little doubt that Houston understood the value of the defense.

Houston also knew from the captured documents that Santa Anna anticipated reinforcements. His brother-in-law, Cós, was coming at some speed. If reinforcements were to arrive, thus bolstering an already larger army, that would also seem to argue for a battle waged from a defensive position. The opposite also had to be considered. Why wait? If Cós was on his way, why not seize the opportunity while enemy force was still at its smallest?

Finally, there was one more consideration. Houston had no way of knowing if Cós was the only reinforcement available to Santa Anna. Days before, he had known the location of Ramírez y Sesma and Filisola, but where were they now? Also, where was Urrea, perhaps Santa Anna's ablest commander? Could not he have been given orders, unknown to Houston, to force march in order to join Santa Anna in the Lynchburg-Anahuac vicinity?

Every subsequent act by Houston would seem to indicate that enemy reinforcement was a major factor in his mind.

In any event, the matter was moot on the morning of April 21, for reconnaissance again brought word that Cós had arrived. Nicholas Lynch, in Henry Millard's command, clearly saw movement through his spyglass. He even saw individual pack mules. That meant that Santa Anna now had perhaps as many as 1,250 men, many of them fresh. Houston had between 743 and 900.

As controversy plagued the entire campaign, it is only fitting that the battle itself be rife with dispute. One of the controversies deals with Vince's Bridge, a timber structure across a creek that produced an estuary in Buffalo Bayou. The bridge, some miles from Lynch's Ferry, lay on the road that led directly to the battlefield. There are those who say that Houston's redoubtable scout, Deaf Smith, had to argue for its destruction. Others contend that someone else, other than Houston, urged its destruction. The most popularly held view, however, is that Houston ordered it destroyed. Anyone who accepts the idea that Houston was plagued by concern over Mexican reinforcements will naturally lean toward the last view. It was obvious that Houston could expect no help, but one thing was certain. Cutting off the only available line of communication, whether for reinforcement or for retreat, stamped on the minds of the Texans the inescapable conclusion that the result of the impending battle really would mean victory or death.

By now Houston had set up his order of battle. He placed Sherman's regiment on his left, the point closest to Lynch's Ferry. To Sherman's right, Burleson's unit occupied the greatest part of the center. Immediately to Burleson's right and somewhat forward was the artillery under the overall supervision of George W. Hockley. Next came more infantry commanded by Henry Millard, who held, essentially, the right flank. Houston avoided having this flank exposed by placing to the very far right and somewhat away from the main body some sixty horsemen under Lamar, partially concealed by a small stand of live oak and brush in front. Santa Anna's order of battle was indistinct, but similar to Houston's. He tried, for example, to maintain cavalry on his somewhat exposed left flank.

Shortly after Santa Anna was reinforced, Houston's adjutant general, John Wharton, moved up and down the line offering words of encouragement and adding all the while that there was nothing to be done but to attack and to attack at once. According to eyewitness Labadie, his words were, "Boys, there is no other word today but fight, fight! Now is the time." It appears that Wharton's insistence succeeded in getting under Houston's skin. Noon came and left, and no order was given, so Wharton took it upon himself to instruct his commander. The content of that conversation will never be known, but Houston's attitude was clear. His last terse sentence thrown in Wharton's face was, "Fight and be damned!"

At this point Houston did something that he had never done before. He held a council of war. Those present included Joseph Bennett, Edward Burleson, Henry Millard, Thomas Rusk, Alexander Somerwell, Sidney Sherman, and Lysander Wells. It is worth noting that John Wharton was not included. Houston gave no indication as to his own preference but informally polled these officers as to their judgments. Should the Texans attack or should they defend? The results indicated a split vote of five to two or four to two, the majority favoring defense. There is no certainty as to Rusk's opinion, but the only two who clearly favored the attack were Bennett and Wells, who also happened to be the lowest-ranking officers present. Even Sherman's vote did not favor the attack. Despite the vote, the men of the army seemed determined to march forth to meet the enemy, and Wharton continued his unsolicited agitation.

By mid-afternoon Santa Anna was convinced that the Texans would not attack. Accordingly, without apparent concern, he decided that it would be a good idea to let Cós's weary troops spend the day at rest. Then, on the morrow, relaxed and refreshed, his force would assault Houston's position, which he viewed as untenable because the Texans had the bayou to their back, the river to their left, and only the open land to their right—

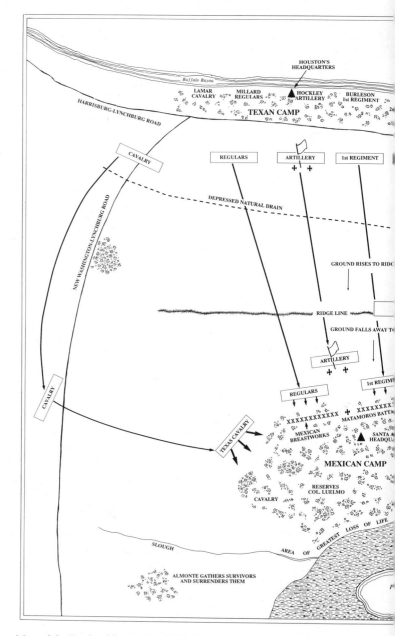

Map of the Battle of San Jacinto by W. T. Kendall and Ronna Hurd.
Courtesy San Jacinto Museum of History.

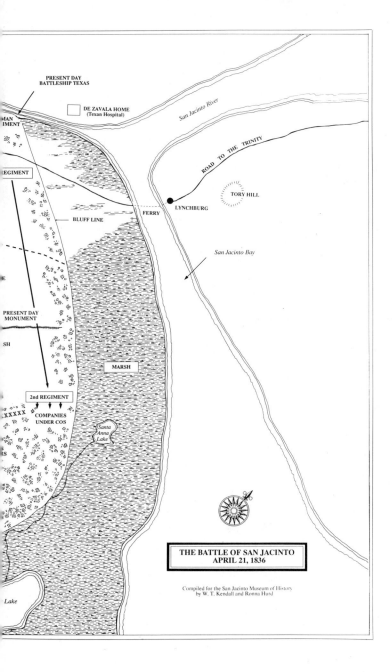

PRESENT DAY
BATTLESHIP TEXAS

DE ZAVALA HOME
(Texan Hospital)

MAN
IMENT

San Jacinto River

REGIMENT

ROAD TO THE TRINITY

BLUFF LINE

FERRY   LYNCHBURG

TORY HILL

San Jacinto Bay

PRESENT DAY
MONUMENT

SH

MARSH

2nd REGIMENT

XXXXX   COMPANIES
UNDER COS

Santa
Anna
Lake

RS

Lake

THE BATTLE OF SAN JACINTO
APRIL 21, 1836

Compiled for the San Jacinto Museum of History
by W. T. Kendall and Ronna Hurd

35

the Texans' only chance of escape as he saw it. By now he also knew that his enemy would be outnumbered. Santa Anna, with his usual confidence, was certain that he could cut them off and could enjoy the leisurely execution of the stragglers as they fled on foot. In a self-satisfied mood, he retired to his tent, secure in the knowledge that all was in order. Perhaps he indulged in his habit of taking opium. Or perhaps, as legend has it, he spent his moments with a mulatto beauty named Emily Morgan (or Emily West as the case may be). In any event he relaxed, and so, apparently, did his troops. It was the hour of siesta, and there appeared to be no threat from the Texans.

If one characteristic in Santa Anna's psyche may be described as his fatal flaw, it would be his overconfidence. To cite only one flagrant example, on April 21 he posted no guards. Later he would blame his subordinates for that failure, but the matter must finally rest at Santa Anna's feet. In the face of an enemy drawn up in line of battle and no more than a thousand yards away, the commander of any army cannot escape the responsibility of seeing to it that, at the very minimum, pickets are provided and battle stations are assigned.

The battlefield today is rather well preserved but a bit confusing. The great monument, a huge obelisk, that commemorates the fight stands roughly midway between the positions of the adversaries. To the northwest of this massive structure, a giant reflecting pool has been constructed. The Texans may have been aligned at the northwestern end of this basin or even farther back. Unit markers are set up farther back in the shadow of a fringe of live oak trees that currently dot the area. It may be assumed that these markers are fairly accurate because they were placed there in the 1890s by veterans of the battle. On the day of the battle, the Texans had to march over the ground that is today part of the pool. The Mexicans, on the other hand, were at what is today the east side of the monument at a distance of some 300 yards. Furthermore, the bank of the San Jacinto River was much steeper than it is today.

All of these matters are important because they bring us to the question of the nature of the land that made up the front for both adversaries. It is difficult to believe, even without the benefit of sentinels, that the Texans' forward movement would have passed unnoticed. A participant in the battle, William Swearingen, whose account is less examined than others, held that the entire area was rather flat. The question must be: how flat? Most historians believe that the Texan attack went undetected for as long as it did because the Mexicans were in slight defilade behind a rise in the land.

In any case, by 3:30 o'clock in the afternoon (some say 4:00), and despite the impromptu vote of the war council, Houston ordered the assault. Perhaps he was only recognizing the truth. The Texans were going to fight; they would not be restrained. Considering their noisy preparation, one also wonders why the Mexicans could not hear them. Still in line of battle, the little army waited for a sign from its commander. Houston drew his sword and motioned the units forward. They emerged from the timber line, each of the large units in column and the soldiers at trail arms and in file. After covering roughly half the distance in this fashion, the units fanned to produce a linear formation consisting of two lines that stretched perhaps 900 yards. At this time the soldiers were ordered to raise their weapons to the port position. Military music, supplied by three fifes and a drum beaten by a free black from New Orleans, began an uncomplicated tune based on a popular song of the day, "Will You Come to the Bower I Have Shaded for You." The beat of the music provided a cadence so that the long line would remain even and there would be no stragglers.

Remarkably, the Mexicans were completely unprepared for the assault. Without adequate security, some dozed in the late afternoon sun, some chatted, and others ate. It was Colonel Pedro Delgado who seems first to have noticed the threat. Quickly a bugle trumpeted a call to stations. General Manuel Fernandez Castrillón, an able soldier who later would be maligned by Santa Anna, realized instantly the gravity of the situation and shouted for a defense. This cry roused some of the lethargic soldiers, but many of the Mexicans continued to lie about. It still had not registered that the outnumbered Texans were actually assaulting their position.

General Sam Houston by Stephen Seymour Thomas, 1892. Oil on canvas, 12 x 9 feet. *Courtesy San Jacinto Museum of History.*

As the drum beat a rough quickstep, the Texans moved swiftly across the field. Apart from the few men with United States Army experience who were present, the Texan force was composed primarily of undisciplined and hastily drilled volunteers. Very few had bayonets. That weapon was particularly suited for the assault, and its scarcity was one of the telling arguments against the attack that was made at the council of war. As the adrenaline pumped through the Texans, the quickstep deteriorated. Soon the men broke into a trot, and the parallel lines sloppily merged into one great mass.

Sam Houston, astride his great white stallion, Saracen, about twenty yards forward of the front ranks, knew that he had little control over these frenzied men; but he was able to stop them long enough for one standing volley to be fired against the enemy lines at a distance of sixty to seventy yards. Even that simple maneuver was too much for Sherman's command, which could not be restrained, and the left flank discharged its weapons indiscriminately. The outraged Houston roared across the field, "Hold your fire, G-- d---you, hold your fire!" This command applied only to those with shoulder and hand weapons, for their effective range was, at best, less than 100 yards. Houston wanted every shot to count. But at this stage, even the normally self-effacing Rusk could not abide a formal battle; at a full gallop, riding hard for the left flank, he yelled in a harsh voice, "If we stop we are cut to pieces. Don't stop—go forward—give them hell!" Some of the Texans had time to reload and refire, but by that time all semblance of linear order had disappeared and a general melee began. Brave Castrillón, faithful to the end, attempted a counterassault, but it was too late.

For the next fifteen minutes, blood and carnage ruled. No one was exempt. Even Houston had two horses shot from under him, including Saracen, and was wounded. With cries of "Remember the Alamo!" and "Remember Goliad!" the bloody-eyed Texans killed as many as they could. It is reported that José Antonio Menchaca, a sergeant and one of the revolutionary Tejanos in the company of Captain Juan Seguin, took up the cry in Spanish, "Recuerden el Alamo!" Seguin, who was promoted to lieutenant

The Battle of San Jacinto by Henry McArdle, 1898. Oil on canvas 92 × 167 inches. *Courtesy Archives Division, Texas State Library.*

Battle of San Jacinto, Texas, by L. M. D. Guillaume, ca. 1892. Oil on canvas, 24 1/4 x 48 inches. Courtesy of the R. W. Norton Art Gallery, Shreveport, La.

Juan Seguin by Thomas Jefferson Wright, 1836. Oil on canvas, 26 1/2 x 24 1/4 inches. *Courtesy Archives Division, Texas State Library.*

colonel after the battle, had been an early opponent of Santa Anna's tyranny and had fought with Jim Bowie at Concepción.

In an attempt to escape the mounting fury, some of Santa Anna's troops, mustering the best English at their disposal, responded in pathetic terror, "Me no Alamo! Me no Goliad!" In some cases, their plaintive appeals may have been true, for many of the men in Cós's command were new replacements. Nevertheless, this was hardly the time for Texan reflection, not in the fever and frenzy of battle. Noah Smithwick, the brawny blacksmith from Gonzales, remembered that Sherman's command, in particular, was "thirsting for gore."

Much of the Mexican defense was lost when its cannon was taken. Realizing its importance, General Castrillón rushed to the cannon and directed its fire as best he could. It managed to get off three rounds but was silenced when the Twin Sisters found its range. At that point, the cannoneers fled, but Castrillón held his place and raised a defiant shout. Rusk did his best to save him, but he was too late. The charging Texans cut him down where he stood.

Colonel Delgado was more fortunate. Sensing all was lost he fled, not toward the obvious escape route to the west or south, but rather to the east and the vicinity of the San Jacinto River. His way took him through the live oaks and into the marshland adjacent to it. In his rush, his boots became mired in the muck and were sucked from his feet. Still, he ran until he came to a body of water that seemingly stopped his progress. Undeterred, he plunged in, together with others who had arrived at the same spot. Simultaneously, Texas riflemen appeared and began to pick off the escapees, but Delgado was saved by the timely arrival of Major John M. Allen. Colonel Juan Almonte, whose mercy had spared Mrs. Burnet, was also spared, and he also lived to tell of it.

Sam Houston, as appalled as anyone at the continuing slaughter, gave orders that the killing should cease, but he was ignored. He is reported to have cried out in desperation, "Gentlemen! Gentlemen! Gentlemen! Gentlemen! I applaud your bravery, but damn your manners!" The battle was over, according to Houston's report, in a mere eighteen minutes, the issue apparently never in doubt; but the killing went on for more than an hour. Houston still had anxious moments even though the victory seemed complete. A grimace of pain creased his face as the blood from his leg wound flowed out of his boot, but he refused all aid. He wanted to see the matter through, and his eyes continually turned to the west, scanning the horizon, trying to determine his next move. He knew that he must have order, so he repeatedly called out the command that was supposed to restore it: "Parade! Parade! Parade! Parade!" It did no good. A careful student of war, Houston knew that defeat could be snatched from the jaws of victory in the twinkling of an eye. Remembering his own

43

Mexican battle flag captured at the Battle of San Jacinto. 44 $^{1}/_{2}$ x 39 $^{1}/_{2}$ inches. *Courtesy Dallas Historical Society.*

military experiences, he also knew the value of a forced march. That meant a rapid strike could very well place Filisola's column in this general area.

It is understandable, then, that when he saw the clearly distinguishable form of Mexican soldiers trooping in the distance, their distinctive tall shako hats bobbing up and down, he feared the worst. According to Captain Amasa Turner, the New Englander who commanded a company, Houston exclaimed, "All is lost!" As it turned out, it was a Mexican troop all right, but it was not the advance guard of a reinforcing column. It was, instead, a large group of prisoners, rounded up and corralled by Rusk, who was bringing them back to camp. These prisoners were the soldiers of the famous Guerrero battalion that had been commanded by Almonte, whose battle flag was captured in the field. The flag remains intact to this day.

Later in the evening, Houston returned to the Texan camp. By that time his wound was aggravated, and he felt considerable pain. Content that the battle was finally over, he allowed his leg to be examined. The ball had struck his lower leg and broken two bones just above his right ankle. It also had sliced his Achilles tendon, and he would always have a slight limp as a souvenir of the day. Even at rest, however, the possibility of an enemy surprise was never far from his mind. Calling for Almonte, he posed two questions: where was Filisola and where was Santa Anna? Almonte in honesty could answer only vaguely. He didn't know, but he had seen Santa Anna riding from the battle just as it appeared that all was lost. The news was a blow to Houston, who understood better than anyone present that the seizure of the Mexican president would be an invaluable asset in bringing the entire war to a successful conclusion. At first glance, the battle seemed decisive, but that was only in a tactical sense. The Mexicans lost enormously in total casualties, while the Texan losses were light. But the battle would not be strategically important if the Mexicans could regain their momentum, and Santa Anna was the key to that.

Several Mexican riders had been seen spurring their horses from the field at the time of the battle. The observant scout Henry Karnes noted the flight and called for volunteers to take up pursuit. One of his comrades in the chase was Deaf Smith. Their search was rewarded, for on April 22 Santa Anna was captured. He had left his worn horse and had moved afoot into the marshland in the direction of Vince's Bridge. Half sloshing, half swimming, he fell exhausted, spending the night lying in the reeds and grass. In the morning he continued his furtive way, but he was soon lost and actually moved toward the Texan camp. He was grateful enough to find some shabby but dry clothing in a slave's quarters. He no longer looked the part of the generalissimo when he was discovered, although he still wore his elegant but dirty shirt complete with diamond studs. Back in the Texan camp, he was greeted with cries of "El Presidente" from his troops. Despite his efforts to silence them, he was recognized and was forthwith brought before Houston, who, still in pain, reclined in the open air beneath a large tree.

The Surrender of Santa Anna by William Henry Huddle, 1890. Oil on canvas, 71 x 113 inches. *Courtesy Archives Division, Texas State Library.*

Texas Veterans of the Battle of San Jacinto at a reunion, date and location unknown. *Courtesy Archives Division, Texas State Library.*

Santa Anna demanded the courtesy he had denied others at the Alamo and Goliad—that he be treated honorably as a prisoner of war. He was, by that time, encircled by wrathful Texans, many of whom wanted his death. Santa Anna visibly trembled in anticipation of his fate, but he need not have worried—Sam Houston had other plans for him. At length, the vain but pleading prisoner gave a brief pompous oration before his crippled captor. His words had to be translated by Almonte: "That man may consider himself born to no common destiny who has captured the Napoleon of the West; and it now remains for him to be generous to the vanquished." Houston's terse reply was that Santa Anna should have remembered that bromide at the Alamo. Santa Anna continued that he was only operating under the orders of his government. Houston correctly pointed out that, as dictator, Santa Anna was the government of Mexico and reminded him as well of the massacre at Goliad. At the mention of that hideous act, Santa Anna blanched but, again, sought to evade responsibility.

Despite the wishes of some of his more outspoken men, Houston had no intention of executing his bloody-handed prisoner. Apart from his natural unwillingness to kill a helpless man, he knew something else—Santa Anna was worth much more to

Texas alive than dead. This wisdom was attested to by the Treaties of Velasco signed by President Burnet and President Santa Anna less than a month after the battle of San Jacinto. That document stated that hostilities would cease and never be renewed, that Mexican troops would be removed from Texas soil, and that the Rio Grande would mark the boundary between the Republic of Texas and Mexico. Even though the Mexican government later declared the treaty null and void, by sparing Santa Anna and by requiring his support, Sam Houston established not only a Texas *de facto* but also a Texas *de jure*.

There are those who maintain that the Battle of San Jacinto need never have been fought. Those who hold this opinion believe that troops of the United States Army, stationed across the Sabine River, ultimately would have saved the situation for the Texans. That is an intriguing view but one that can never be proven conclusively.

There is no question that the Battle of San Jacinto was decisive in the tactical sense. Indeed, few victories have been more complete. In the strategic sense, however, it may have been another matter, for Sam Houston's little army had beaten only the force under Santa Anna. The main Mexican army still remained under the command of Filisola, and it would have to be dealt with. True, its supplies were stretched, but it was still able to carry on the war for a time at least. Filisola, however, obeyed Santa Anna's order to leave Texas, and it was that act that ended the revolution.

As to the battle itself and its results, it would be difficult indeed to improve upon what is written on the base of the great monument that marks its site: "Measured by its results, San Jacinto was one of the decisive battles of the world. The freedom of Texas from Mexico won here led to annexation and to the Mexican War, resulting in the acquisition by the United States of the states of Texas, New Mexico, Arizona, Nevada, California, Utah, and parts of Colorado, Wyoming, Kansas, and Oklahoma. Almost one-third of the present area of the American nation, nearly a million square miles, changed sovereignty."

About the Author

James W. Pohl is a historian specializing in military history. He received his B.A. and M.A. degrees from the University of North Texas and his Ph.D. in history from the University of Texas at Austin. He has published widely on military topics, and serves as an advisory editor for the new *Handbook of Texas*. Dr. Pohl is a former president of the Texas State Historical Association and is a professor of history at Southwest Texas State Universitry in San Marcos.